Enter
My
Mind

Shauna Cesar

DEDICATION

To all who have helped me get through my formative years
in one piece. My family for always being there and my
friends who kept me busy.

CONTENTS

Warning

Welcome to my mind from preteen to young adult. Going through the onset of bi-polar disorder without having a clue as to why I thought and felt the way I did I escaped through my poetry. A lot of it is far from being considered happy or even appealing. But I have the comfort in knowing that I am not the only one who has had thoughts like this at one point in time or another.

I am one of the least violent people anyone will ever meet. I do not condone violence or self-harm. I do however encourage if someone has similar thoughts to find a harmless outlet for it. Poetry was and is mine.

Yesterday

I am a day
not a weekday
or weekend

Gone and
Unchangeable

Unmemorable unless
exciting, sad
or interesting

Without attention
I am lifeless
disappearing
into shadows

Only known in
pictures and stories
unnoticed
until forgotten

Fairytales

Remember as a young child

Prince charming

On white horses

And one sentence

Happily ever after

It won't happen

Remember as an older child

Dreams of being in movies

Husbands and children

And one sentence

Happily ever after

It hardly happens

Remember as a naive youngster

Happiness everlasting

Forever-unbroken promises

And one sentence

Happily ever after

It won't happen

Do you believe in fairytales?

A young child

Once did
And one sentence

Happily ever after

Nothing like this ever happens

Keep remembering

Give it up

Move on

Darkness

While surrounded in depression, no matter how untrue, no one likes you and no one can be trusted. It is extremely hard to be around people when you are constantly doubting intentions.

The only light in the never-ending darkness is the knowledge that this will come to an end. That is what makes holding on easier.

As They Sit

Please don't let

My classmates find out,

My friends know,

My family tell,

The things I've done!
The thoughts I've had!
The words I've said!

She wonders
Do they know?

He thinks
They have to know!

Paranoia sets in

Darkness comes

Self-loathing takes over
Horrible things happen

Some will make it
Most wont
Will she be lucky?
Will he?

No Where, No One

No where to run
No where to hide

No one to care
No one to die

No where to scream
No where to cry

No one to love
No one to lie

No where to go
To be all alone

No one to be there
To take you home

The Mind

Happiness eludes
Others exclude
No one notices

Thoughts confuse
Paranoia ensues
Everyone excuses

Love enthralls
Above all
Only I care

Honesty's evasive
Openness pervasive
Yet it's needed

Intimacy's jaded
Veneers faded
Nothing helps

Innocence gone
Pessimism won
Rejection's eminent

No One Else

I need you
Here with my despair
To resent my hate
And kill my cry

No one else
Sees what you can

I want you
Doing what you can
To finish what I can't
And drown my depression

No one else
Seems to care

I love you
Make me happy
Show you care
And prove your love

No one else
But me cried

Why?

Light?

Even the light and "happy" days seem to have some sort of impending darkness. That lurking darkness seemed to be more trying on my sanity than being totally engulfed in depression.

It is hard to look forward to your future and be excited about it knowing that it includes dark depressing days and an inability to trust.

One Lone Soul

Inviting
Unlocked
Wide open

Un-passable
Forbidding
Quite hurtful

Silent
Calm
Too peaceful

Untrusting
Violent
So poisonous

One lone soul
One strange person
Confused and torn apart

The Scary Time

Dark clouds enfold me
And I can't stop them
Sadly this isn't the scary time

Weeks wandering around
In a black haze
Wondering if anyone notices

Happiness is coming
It seems to take so long
But it comes

This is the scary time
Feeling so good
Not wanting it to end

Sometimes thinking
It will never end
If I do

But what about my friends
My family
My life

Hoping it ends
Before I decide to

Memories

Remember the sunsets
Watched from the beach
Remember the walks
Barefoot on the sand

Good memories flood the mind
Until they come
Out of nowhere
To over whelm

Remember the fights
Unforgotten words
Remember the break-up
Then comes the end

Bad memories from the soul
In mind and dreams
Until the apology
New one begins, old one ends

Remember the flowers
Sent with deep love
Remember the candle light dinner
To mark yet another year

Good memories true to heart
Some fade others stay
Love needed
To stay sane

Remember the walk out
Never to come back
Remember no where to stay
Love taken away

Bad memories truth to hurt
Cruel comments, harsh fight
Unforgotten personality
Forgotten heart, soul, and love

Do To Me

Scream
Please scream for me
That's why I do this
Chills knowing
I caused that

Does it hurt
When I do this
Are you scared
Of the blood
I'm not

In the end
It's not worth it
The questions
The scars Reminders

Of what I do to me

Shauna Cesar

Life And Death

While growing up a lot of my time was spent thinking of death and convoluted ideas of what my life was destined to be. With paranoia about all people in general this made for some very dark depressing thoughts on the future and what people are capable of.

Sickness and Death

Life, a broken winged bird
Cannot move or fly
Just left behind
In sickness and death

Ready to die alone
With wishes of flight
Far from this place
That reeks of death

With no one to care
It slowly melts away
Losing all chances of flight
At the end of life's days

Trust No One

The stiff embrace
Urgent desire
Moist smoky breath
No questions

Why let this woman
See through tomorrow
Be her universe

Her dark translucent eyes
Broken free but
Who will remember
Never open up

Blood Red

Blood red eyes
Blood curdling screams

Blood red fire
Red sash tied too tight

Blood red wine
Blood rushing from the face

Blood red knife
Red shirt once white

Blood red puddle
Blood trail as he ran

Numb

Jukebox is singing
CD is spinning
My heart is swinging
And I don't know why

Music is pumping
My head is thumping
Thinking of something
But I don't know what

The feeling of falling
My warm bed is calling
But this guy is stalling
And I don't know why

Is that blood running
My body is numbing
Something is coming
But I don't know what

Shauna Cesar

Parenthood/Children

Becoming a parent just at the time I was understanding my disorder was one of the toughest things I have ever gone through. At a time when I was learning how to control strange thoughts it was extremely scary thinking about having to put an innocent life into the situation.

I love my children above anything and I have them to thank for my quick understanding and brute determination to write it out and get it out of my head.

She

She smiles
While she cries

She is happy
With her pain

She loves
Her discomfort

She doesn't cringe
When she screams

She laughs
As she bleeds

She's full of joy
When she sweats

There is a new cry
In the room
It all starts to make sense

A Depressed Parents Prayer

I hope my children never
See the horrors
Feel the pain
Do the things
I have

I hope my children never
Inflict the pain
Create the horrors
Do the things
I have

Please don't let them
See me cry
Every night
Feel the scars
From my insides

Please don't let me
Pain their hearts
With my sadness
Scar their futures
With my tears

Guide Me

Perhaps silently
The broken lights save
For the fog does guide

Descend these stairs
And understand
Eyes cloaked
In shadows guide

Shauna Cesar

The End?

And now we come to the end. I would like to thank you for making it this far.

Rather than going on and on I will leave you with one last poem. One of the most controversial poems I have written. I wrote this at the ripe young age of 14 and the first time it was read I was asked if I needed help. The answer then was no but looking back it should have been yes.

Suicide

Walking into the house
Such a long day
So exhausted
Life so complicated
Don't know what to do anymore
World so violent
Life going nowhere
Life not worth it
No where to run and hide
End it all

BANG

With ever climbing statistics of mental health issues in teenagers throughout the world there are plenty of resources available if you are looking for help. I implore each and every person who may be struggling with dark thoughts, sadness, or even just a feeling that something just isn't right to reach out and find that help.

Have a person you can tell anything without judgments, talk to your doctor, or even just find a personal way to express yourself to get it out. If at any time you have the urge or serious thoughts about hurting yourself or others find professional help.

Violence in any way is not the answer. There is always another option. There is always a choice so please make the choice that will change for the better.

If you know someone that shows signs of mental health issues please reach out and help them.

Help Lines

Here are the help lines I could find as of the date of publication, if the numbers have changed please feel free to contact me so I can change it.

Canada

Emergency Medical: 911

Mental Health Help Line British Columbia
    310-6789 or 1800-SUICIDE

Mental Health Help Line Alberta
    1-877-303-2642

Saskatchewan Suicide Help Line
    Regina: 306-525-5333
    Prince Albert: 306-764-1011
    Saskatoon: 306-933-6200

Manitoba Suicide Prevention and Support Line
    1-877-531-2600

Mental Health Help Line Ontario
    1-866-531-2600

Suicide Action Montreal (English & French)
    1-866-277-3553

Mental Health Mobile Crisis Nova Scotia
    1-888-429-8167

Chimo Help Line New Brunswick
1-800-667-5005

The Island Help Line P.E.I
1-800-218-2885

Yukon Distress and Support Line
1-800-563-0808

The N.W.T Help Line
1-800-661-0844

Nunavut Kamatsiaqtut Help Line
1-800-265-3333

Kids Help Phone Canada
1-800-668-6868

USA

Emergency Medical: 911

National Suicide Prevention Lifeline
1-800-273-TALK (8255)

SAMHSA Treatment Referral Helpline
1-877-726-4727